50 LONDON BUILDINGS

By Harry Palmer

SHANE BOOKS

First published in 2022 by

Shane Books,
Flat 1, No. 21 The Ridgeway,
Enfield,
Middlesex. EN2 8NX

ISBN: 978-1-9160230-5-5

CONTENTS

1.

HOUSE 1726-1728

4 St. James Square SW1
By Edward Shepherd

5
IN
OUT

2.

HIGHGATE CEMETERY STARTED 1838

Swains Lane N6
by Stephen Geary, J. B. Bunning and J. Oldred Scott

GOLDHAMMER

3.

ROYAL EXCHANGE 1841-1844

Threadneedle Street EC3
by William Tite

THE
ROYAL

4.

LEOPOLD BUILDINGS

Columbia Road E2
by H. A. Darbishire

RA57 WZS

5.

ST. PANCRAS INTERNATIONAL 1866-1868
HOTEL AND OFFICES 1868-1876

Euston Road NW1
by George Gilbert Scott

ELL 4X

6.

ROYAL ALBERT HALL 1867

Kensington Gore SW7
by Francis Fowke

7.

ROYAL COLLEGE OF ORGANISTS 1875

Kensington Gore SW7
by H. H. Cole

8.

STUDIO HOUSE 1875-1876

8 Melbury Road W14
by Richard Norman Shaw

STONE
POWELL

9.

GIBSON GARDENS 1880

Stoke Newington N16
Built by the Metropolitan Association for Improving the Dwellings of the Industrious Classes

10.

BROMPTON ORATORY 1880-1893

Brompton Road SW3
by Herbert Gribble

ELEGI ET
SANCTI
FICAVI
LOC
S.FELIX

11.

COLBECK MEWS NO'S 1-6 1883-1884

by Ernest George & Peto architects

12.

PRUDENTIAL ASSURANCE 1895-1901

High Holborn EC1
by Alfred Waterhouse

13.

37 HARLEY STREET 1897-1899

W1G
by Arthur Beresford Pite

QUEEN ANNE
STREET W1

14.

FIRE STATION 1901-1902

Euston Road NW1
LCC Architects Department: W. E. Riley

L.C.C. FIRE BRIGADE STATION EUSTON 1902

15.

THE BLACK FRIAR 1904

Queen Victoria Street EC4
by H. Fuller Clark

174

16.

WORKING MEN'S COLLEGE 1905

Crowndale Road NW1
by W. H. Caro

WORKING · MEN'S · COLLEGE

17.

DEBENHAM HOUSE 1905-1907

8 Addison Road W14
by Halsey Ricardo

18.

CONNAUGHT ROOMS, 1905-1910

Great Queen Street, WC2B
by Alexander Brown and Ernest Barrow

19.

BROMPTON ROAD UNDERGROUND STATION 1906

Cottage Place SW3
by Leslie W. Green

20.

ST. IGNATIUS CHURCH 1911

27 High Road, Stamford Hill N15
by Benedict Williamson

21.

EX PORT OF LONDON AUTHORITY 1912

10 Trinity Square EC3
by Edwin Cooper

22.

30A AND 30B WIMPOLE STREET 1912

by Bannister Fletcher & Sons

WIMPOLE
STREET W1
NEW CAVENDISH
STREET W1

23.

EX DAIMLER CAR HIRE GARAGE 1931

Herbrand Street WC1
by Wallis, Gilbert and Partners

24.

HOOVER BUILDING, WESTERN AVENUE, PERIVALE

by Wallis, Gilbert & Partners

25.

ISOKON FLATS 1933

Lawn Road NW3
by Wells Coates

26.

22 WEYMOUTH STREET, W1G 1934

by Giles Gilbert Scott

LX67 NHB

27.

THE PANTILES 1934-1935

Finchley Road, Temple Fortune, Barnet
by J. B. F. Cowper

28.

DORSET HOUSE 1935

Gloucester Place and Marylebone Road NW1
by T. P. Bennett with Joseph Emberton

DORSET HOUSE
DORSET HOUSE

Londis

29.

PINNER COURT 1935-1936

Pinner Road, North Harrow
by H. J. Mark

30.

HIGHPOINT I & II 1935-1938

High Hill, Highgate
by Berthold Lubetkin

31.

KENT HOUSE 1936

Ferdinand Street NW1
by Connell, Ward and Lucas

KENT HOUSE
Bruce
Offices
LET BY
anise

32.

CONGRESS HOUSE 1953-1960

Great Russell Street WC1
by David du R. Aberdeen

TRADES UNION CONGRESS
TUC

33.

BEVIN COURT 1954

Cruickshank Street, Islington
by Skinner, Bailey & Lubetkin

34.

BARBICAN ESTATE, 1959-1979

Beech Street, Moorgate and Aldersgate Street EC1, EC2
by Chamberlin, Powell and Bon

35.

MARATHON HOUSE, EX CASTROL HOUSE 1960

174 Marylebone Road NW1
by Gollings, Melvin, Ward and Partners

36.

78 SOUTH HILL PARK 1963-1965

NW3
Designed by Brian Housden

37.

WINSCOMBE STREET 1965

22-32 Winscombe Street, Camden
by Neave Brown

30

38.

BRUNSWICK CENTRE 1965-1973

designed by Patrick Hodgkinson

UBER
EATS

39.

EX PADDINGTON MAINTENANCE DEPOT 1966-1968

179 Harrow Road W2
by Bicknell & Hamilton

40.

MARQUESS ESTATE 1966-1976

Canonbury N1
Designed by Geoffrey Darbourne and John Darke

41.

HAYWARD GALLERY, BELVEDERE ROAD SE1 1967

Designed by Greater London Council Architect's Department

HAYWARD GALLERY
HAYWARD GALLERY
Matthew Barney

42.

INGESTRE ROAD ESTATE 1967-1971

Kentish Town, NW5
Designed by John Green for Camden Architects' Department

43.

CENTRAL HILL ESTATE 1970-1974

Hawke Road, Lambeth
by Rosemary Stjernstedt

44.

BRANCH HILL ESTATE, SPEDAN CLOSE 1970-1977

Hampstead NW3
by Gordon Benson and Alan Forsyth for Camden Architects' Department

45.

DUNBOYNE ROAD ESTATE 1971-1977

Dunboyne Road, NW3
Designed by Neave Brown for Camden Architects' Department

46.

THAMESMEAD, LONDON SE2 STARTED 1972

Designed by GLC Department of Architecture Phase 1 designed by Philip Bottomley

47.

TRELLICK TOWER 1973

Golborn Road W10
by Ernö Goldfinger

TRELLICK TOWER

48.

MAIDEN LANE ESTATE 1979-1982

St. Paul's Crescent, Camden NW1
Designed by Alan Forsyth and Gordon Benson
for Camden Architects' Department

49.

NO. 1 POULTRY 1994-1998

Poultry and Queen Victoria Street EC2
by James Stirling and Michael Wilford

50.

HOUSE, COTTAGE PLACE 2012

SW3
by Chipperfield Architects

ALSO AVAILABLE FROM SHANE BOOKS

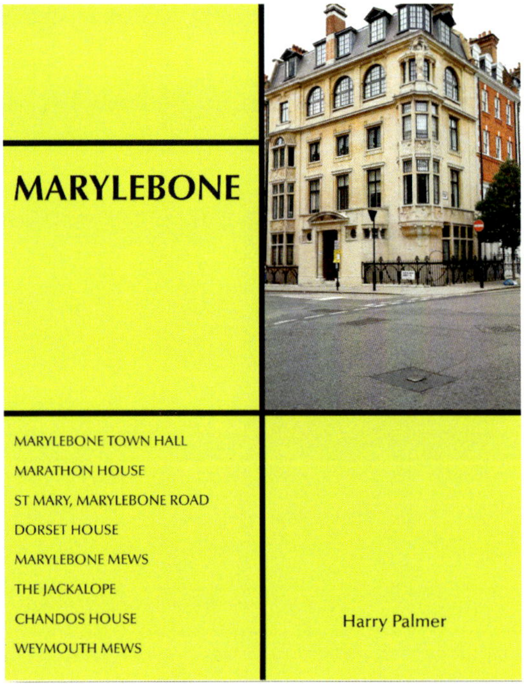